ITALY

A PICTURE MEMORY

Text
Bill Harris

Photography
Colour Library Books Ltd.
The Telegraph Colour Library

Captions
Fleur Robertson

Editorial
Fleur Robertson

Design
Teddy Hartshorn

Director of Production
Gerald Hughes

CLB 2794
© 1992 CLB Publishing, Godalming, Surrey, England
All rights reserved.
This 1993 edition published by Magna Books,
Magna Road, Wigston, Leicester, England
Colour separations by Scantrans Pte Ltd, Singapore
Printed and bound by Tien Wah Press (PTE) Ltd, Singapore
ISBN 1-85422-550-2

ITALY
A PICTURE MEMORY

MAGNA BOOKS

First page: the Roman Forum in Rome, and (previous pages) the silhouette of Venice's Santa Maria della Salute at sunset.

"I'm bored with Venice," he said.

Incredible as it may sound, a professional traveler recently made that confession on national television, in a travelogue on Italy, no less. If you didn't turn off your set right there, you would have been treated to images of hill towns and villages which, like Venice herself, are capable of inspiring any number of wonderful emotions. But never boredom. You would also have been told, to the point of boredom, that these places are in great danger of losing their charm once the "tourists" discover them.

It is a fact that at some times of the year Italy's foreign visitors seem to outnumber the Italians themselves, that tourism pumps some nine trillion lire into the country's economy annually and that the numbers are growing fast. There is hardly a corner of the peninsula they haven't long since discovered, but the Italians don't worry that foreigners are going to ruin the place. They haven't succeeded yet and they've been arriving in sometimes alarming numbers since the Greeks began visiting the Etruscans five hundred years or so before the birth of Christ.

The Greeks could hardly be called tourists. They decided to stay, in fact, and even after the Romans finally drove them out they left behind the notion of the city-state that survived among the Italians until the late nineteenth century, when a dozen independent kingdoms were finally united. Technically, the separate kingdoms had been kept apart all that time by foreign powers with a divide-and-conquer mentality, but Italians even today are generally more attached to their cities than to the republic, even if they hail from small towns. A cookbook writer may get enthusiastic about the cuisine of Liguria, but the people who grew up with it will call it Genovese. And although they are fellow Italians, a native of Genoa still feels vaguely superior to a Venetian, as if the two former city-states were still competing as great maritime powers.

Considering the long centuries of interference from just about every foreign power in the world, it's incredible that regional loyalty is still so deep among Italians. And it's equally incredible that they never picked up the customs and habits of the foreigners. One theory is that the other civilizations were created by wandering rural people who didn't understand the psychological importance of cities and ignored them in favor of capturing large territories, which left the Italian people able to keep aloof from the conquerors behind their city walls. And it is interesting that, except for fortifications designed to keep them out, there aren't many physical reminders of foreign invaders in Italy, even though they divided it up among themselves for centuries.

Ironically, the only real monuments to outsiders in Italy are the Greek ruins in Sicily and the South, possibly grander than those in Greece itself. Yet most attempts to explain away the fact that Italy will probably always be divided into North and South – as different from one another as two separate countries - begin with tales of foreign influences from the other side of the Alps. It's true that most invaders rarely went further south than Rome, but Rome itself is probably more responsible. Unification became a reality when the Royal Italian Army marched into Rome on September 20, 1870, but until that day the Church had control over a wide swath of territory that cut the Italian Peninsula neatly in two. Only the Kingdoms of Naples and Sicily were south of it and for hundreds of years they were not involved in many of the cultural and political events that affected their cousins in the North. As one of their kings proudly noted, "My kingdom is an island, protected by salt water on three sides and holy water on the other." Even unification really didn't unite them – it wasn't until the railroads arrived that anyone at either end of Italy seemed to notice that there were Italians at the other end.

But if Northern Italians came by their outlook on life learning to survive with foreigners in their midst, the Southerners achieved something similar fighting a hostile environment. As attractive as "Sunny Italy" may seem to vacationers, lack of rain has always made life in the South a tough proposition. The result is that there are more similarities among the natives of the two Italys than even they are willing to admit. But clichés abound.

In the North, where many consider Southerners generally shiftless and witless, they whisper of a feudal society run by petty officials who operate outside the law, frequently terrorize their neighbors and would rather have power than wealth. To a Milanese, to whom money often seems to be the root of all power, such men are a drag on the society. On the other hand, the Neapolitans look northward and see insufferable egoists so busy amassing wealth that they forget to take the time to enjoy life, and they say that is an unpardonable sin in Italy of all places. Fortunately, the society has survived in spite of all the whispering and no one seriously believes that any Italian, Northern or Southern, doesn't know how to enjoy life.

That joy was among the things that attracted the first waves of foreign "tourists" near the end of the seventeenth century. The end of the Thirty Years' War in 1648 made travel in Europe comparatively safe and the idea of the Grand Tour was born. It was a way for the aristocracy to flaunt its wealth and its abundance of leisure time. The stated purpose was to give young men of good families a more rounded outlook on life, to expose them to better manners and better fashions and to give them membership in a kind of culture club. The journeys typically lasted a year or longer. There would be long stays in Paris to stuff their heads with the ideas of the Englightenment and to stuff their already heavy trunks with modish clothes. Then they would go off to Vienna to hear the latest music, to Amsterdam for a first-hand look at the work of the Dutch Masters and to the Rhineland to study castles and absorb the legends of the past. The itinerary varied over the years to avoid the dangers of wars that seemed to be cropping up all over the place, but that just heightened the sense of adventure, and when there was no war, there were always brigands and highwaymen to help make a Grand Tour memorable. But wherever the tourists went, they generally reserved Italy for the last stop, like the icing on the cake. The remains of the Roman Empire and the legacy of the Renaissance provided them with the cultural justification for crossing the Alps, but after a year of absorbing the lessons of history and of art, they were usually ready for headier things. The climate was a big lure, of course, but it was the Italian people who gave them something to think about. Most of the tourists arrived with letters of introduction to noble Italian families and what they found as guests in their palazzi was a far cry from the lifestyles they remembered in the manor houses back home.

Not everyone on a Grand Tour was looking for nothing more than to stand where Cicero spoke and to sit at Michelangelo's feet. Many of them came from England where Puritanism was in vogue and what they had on their minds was, in a word, sex. It wasn't easy for them to concentrate on paintings and sculpture when there were dark Latin beauties lurking in the background and their heads were filled with tales of romance carried home by chums who had taken the tour before them. Even the warning of the poet Shelley who had written home: "Young women of rank actually eat ... you'll never guess what ... garlic!" didn't deter them. Their amorous adventures were probably exaggerated, but kiss-and-tell accounts of visits to the land of Casanova may have done more for early Italian tourism than all the museums and galleries put together.

But long before Grand Tours became fashionable Italy had another lure for tourists that transcended art and antiquity and even human contact. Even before the Middle Ages visitors braved the dangers of cosssing the Alps for the privilege of visiting the seat of the Catholic Church and for the opportunity to be blessed by the Pope himself. They faced possible death in unexpected Alpine avalanches or at the hands of bandits, but to encourage them to make the trip, the Church told them that a soul released by death on a pilgrimage was guaranteed escape from the punishment of purgatory.

Millions made the journey, followed in a few years by armies impressed by Papal power and determined to impress the Pope with their own. They were followed in turn by crusaders on their way to Jerusalem, and through it all Italy was less changed than they themselves.

After the fifteenth century, when the Italians began transforming the world's view of itself through the artistic and scientific innovation of the Renaissance, foreigners in even greater numbers began flocking to Italy for a different kind of spiritual uplift. But the opulence that had been created made Italy too tempting to be ignored by the power hungry among them, and the next great wave of outsiders changed the outlook of the Italian people, not to mention the landscape, as no wave of tourists has ever affected any country. It all began when the King of Milan, who had a long-standing dispute with the King of Naples, decided to invite the new King Charles VIII of France to come fight his battles for him. It was an odd request. Charles was universally regarded as a dull man. He had emptied his treasury bribing the English so they would not attack him, turned over his defenses to the Spanish to prove his un-warlike intentions against them and gave whole provinces to the Austrian-based Holy Roman Empire so the Emperor Maximilian wouldn't take more on his own. His army was pitifully weak, but he decided to send it anyway.

There was no resistance anywhere they went. Principality after principality surrendered to the French without a fight. The Florentines welcomed them with open arms and even bribed them to keep on moving south. When they reached Rome, where the people were fed up with the Pope and his relatives, they were hailed as new saviors. And by the time they marched into Naples, the people there were enthusiastically studying French. But they were still Italians and after a few months of watching him raid their treasury and systematically replacing their officials with his own men, they began conspiring with their fellow Italians to send Charles back where he came from. The French king got the message and headed back up the peninsula, but it was too late. The Italian princes had decided that if they let him go home unpunished other armies would be encouraged to follow, and so on July 6, 1495, a combined army of all the Italian kingdoms met the French at the little town of Fornovo. The French were tired and woefully outnumbered and the Italians fresh and well disciplined, but the battle itself was a disaster. More than four thousand men were butchered in less than an hour, more of them Italian than French, and in the end Charles escaped across the Alps with the few soldiers he had left and disappeared into history. It was a humiliating defeat for the Italians, but a victory for the cynics who had been saying that Italy couldn't cope with the idea of unification. It also provided the signal to other powers that the Italians had dreaded all along – for the next three decades Italy was overrun by one or another of them, and the small armies of the independent republics and kingdoms were powerless against them.

The worst humiliation of all was yet to come. In 1527, the largely Spanish army of the Holy Roman Empire, fresh from a victory over the French at Milan, augmented by 12,000 zealous Lutherans with a lust to hang the Pope, and thousands of others who lusted after the Church's treasure, marched on Rome with death and destruction in mind. The battle was shorter than the one at Fornovo, but the death and destruction didn't end with the tearing down of the city's gates. Over the next several months, the conquerors amused themselves ransacking houses and palaces and then setting fire to them. Women were raped and men were tortured. By the time Pope Clement VII paid the demanded ransom for his life and slipped away in disguise, two-thirds of the population of Rome was dead and most of its buildings, from great churches to simple houses, were smoking ruins.

When the smoke cleared, the Spanish were in control and remained the dominant influence on Italian life, along with the Church, for the next century and a half. But the Italians had the last laugh. In the 1600s all of Europe was under the control of rigid monarchies that demanded absolute loyalty. People with ideas of their own were either burned at the stake or chained to the wall of a dungeon. Strict morality was demanded and nonconformity rejected and most Europeans knuckled under. There was no other choice. But the Italians invented one. It was a masterpiece of nonconformity that even the most dull-witted bureaucrats couldn't help loving: Baroque art and architecture. The Italians were defeated and oppressed, but they had a sense of theater that allowed them to rise above the humdrum life that outsiders were trying to impose on them. The Renaissance had made Italy dominant in science and the arts: giants like Michelangelo and Titian, Cellini and Palladio simply picked up where they left off before the Sack of Rome. When they died, they were replaced by the likes of Tintoretto, Veronese and Caravaggio. At first glance they seemed to be following the classical ideas of their predecessors, but something new was added. Color and light and movement gave their works a sense of exuberance and fantasy, and though critics put it all down as absurd and even bizarre, the movement they named for a deformed pearl was an expression of the Italian soul. Architects and sculptors took to the style like ducks to water and created cathedrals and palaces, gardens and town squares that still endure as permanent stage sets. They carried the drama abroad, but their best work was on the home front, especially in the rebuilding of Rome.

The movement went beyond art and architecture. The Italians' retreat into a world of make-believe led to the creation of the Teatro dell'arte, whose strolling players wandered all over Europe improvising as they went along and changing the world's concept of theater itself. The Teatro had its beginnings in sixteenth-century Florence at about the same time that the Florentines were experimenting with a new form, loosely based on Greek drama, where the dialogue was sung rather than spoken. The idea came out of the nobility's private theaters when Claudio Monteverdi became music master at St. Mark's in Venice and found the freedom to perfect the art form. By 1640, his operas were reducing audiences to tears in a half-dozen Venetian theaters and before long there were opera houses in Naples and Milan where the scenery, costumes and stagecraft were as popular as the music itself.

The Italian musical tradition that made immortals of Vivaldi and Pergolesi, Verdi and Puccini began in earnest in 1562 when the princes of the Church decided the time had come to ban music from churches because nearly all of it was based on popular songs that were being sung in taverns and brothels. The ban had some merit, but a mass without music was like a day without sunshine to the Italians and faced with the prospect of empty churches, a committee of cardinals commissioned Giovanni Palestrina to compose music for the mass that would be properly ecclesiastical. To the relief of future generations, he succeeded admirably.

Life among the Italians for the more than two centuries of the Baroque Age was dedicated almost completely to hiding reality, which was unpleasant, behind increasingly elaborate facades, which were glorious. Many outsiders praised and even envied what they called "the fine Italian hand," but hard-nosed realists said that there was no future in art for the sake of rising above one's oppressors.

Oppressors come and go and their names are eventually forgotten. But if all the world is a stage, it would be a much less interesting place if the Italians hadn't designed the sets. And in this modern world where technology has stepped up the pace to the point where psychiatrists have become a necessity, Italy is an oasis in the global village. Life is no less hard for Italians than for anyone else; it's even harder by many standards. But they never cease to charm the visitors who descend on them like locusts in the spring and summer and go home asking themselves, "Why can't we be more like the Italians?" Why, indeed? They invented the art of living long before modern societies created what they like to call traditional values, and if the art is superficial, there is no denying it has stood the test of time; if what foreigners see in Italy is all a facade, the illusion is magical. It dips into the corner of the soul that resents regimentation, rebels against moralism and loves the idea that life is never so oppressive that it can't be shrugged off with a smile, a good meal and a bottle of wine.

And that is why tourists will never ruin Italy. They are too important as part of the show. If they succeed in changing anything, it is their own outlook on life.

Facing page: the Italian Alps in summer.

Below: the landscape around Langkofel, east of Bolzano in the Dolomites (these pages and overleaf), northern Italy. This mountain range is popular with visitors all year; in the winter the skiing here is particularly good, while in the summer the unspoiled countryside is a great attraction. Right: the church of St. Cyprian in Tiers, (below right) secluded Lake Carezza, and (bottom right) Mount Marmarole, the king of the Marmarole Range. Overleaf: a mountain lake near Misurina.

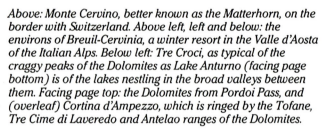

Above: Monte Cervino, better known as the Matterhorn, on the border with Switzerland. Above left, left and below: the environs of Breuil-Cervinia, a winter resort in the Valle d'Aosta of the Italian Alps. Below left: Tre Croci, as typical of the craggy peaks of the Dolomites as Lake Anturno (facing page bottom) is of the lakes nestling in the broad valleys between them. Facing page top: the Dolomites from Pordoi Pass, and (overleaf) Cortina d'Ampezzo, which is ringed by the Tofane, Tre Cime di Laveredo and Antelao ranges of the Dolomites.

Above: Lazise Harbor, and (facing page bottom) Scaligers' Castle, Sirmione, both on Lake Garda (above left and facing page top), one of the primary lakes of the Italian Lakes region. Notable for both its beauty and its size, Lake Garda has been fought over throughout history for its commercial and strategic importance. Left: Lake Valvestino, near Lake Garda. Below left: the Roman arena in Verona, still in use and one of the largest in existence, and (below) the Arch of Peace in Milan, whose superb cathedral (overleaf) dominates the city.

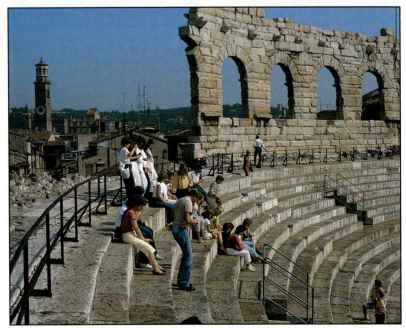

Facing page: the Church of St. George Major, and (above) the Campanile and Basilica of St. Mark's in St. Mark's Square (below and below right), the centerpiece of Venice. The city's major thoroughfare is a waterway, the Grand Canal (above right), along which can be viewed many of Venice's finest buildings, such as Santa Maria Della Salute (right), likened by Henry James to "some great lady on the threshold of her saloon." Overleaf: the Venetian Regatta on the Grand Canal.

Venice (these pages and overleaf) has a cinematic air, nearly every part of it appearing intriguingly old, untouched by this century. Above: a gondolier relaxes before plying his trade on the city's narrow water corridors (below) and on the Grand Canal (below left and left), which passes under the sixteenth-century Rialto Bridge (facing page bottom), one of Venice's most famous bridges. Above left: St. Mark's Square and the Doge's Palace, once the official residence of the mighty rulers of Venice, and (facing page top) Santa Maria della Salute.

The Italian Riviera comprises a strip of coastline between the French border and Tuscany. From Genoa to France it is known as the Riviera di Ponente, and to the east of Genoa as the Riviera di Levante. The latter boasts many fine resorts, such as Rapallo (bottom left), Riomaggiore (left) and Portofino (overleaf), but perhaps the most romantic is Portovenere (below), whence the club-footed English poet, Byron, swam to Lerici (below left) – several miles away – to visit his friend Shelley.

The Leaning Tower of Pisa (below), which at its top is some thirteen feet from the vertical, has defied gravity for over 600 years. Below right: Pisa Cathedral, the first of the black and white Tuscan cathedrals. Pisa was extensively bombed during the Second World War – it was a miracle that the tower and the cathedral were not damaged. Bottom right: Florence's Cathedral and Baptistry standing at the heart of the world's greatest Renaissance city, and (right and overleaf) the center of Siena.

Florence (below left and facing page) is one of the most attractive cities in Italy, its rich, golden brown buildings being set amid low hills in a landscape of cypresses and vineyards. It lies on the River Arno, which is spanned by the Ponte Vecchio (left and below). This old bridge, lined with jeweler's shops, displays a bust of Benvenuto Cellini, the brilliant Florentine goldsmith. Above: the massive marble statue of Neptune by Ammannati, which stands in Florence's Piazza della Signoria (above left) and was sculpted to rival Michelangelo's David.

By day or night, Florence (these pages) is renowned for the beauty of its architecture. The church of San Frediano in Cestello (left) is one of many places of worship situated beside the River Arno (below left). Some of these churches are floodlit at night – the most magnificent being Florence's cathedral (bottom left and overleaf). Below: the Ponte Vecchio, the only bridge left standing when the Germans, fighting a rearguard action against the Allies, destroyed the rest in August 1944.

Facing page top: an Umbrian church in the Spoleto Valley. The Umbrian countryside is comparable in beauty to the finest Tuscan landscapes (facing page bottom) – both remain reminiscent of the views of the region to be seen in the paintings of the Renaissance artists of the fifteenth and sixteenth centuries. Below: the imposingly situated Umbrian hill town of Trevi, which has been in existence since Roman times when was known as Trebiae. *The town boasts a fine fifteenth-century church.*

These pages and overleaf: Rome, the capital city of Italy and once the center of an empire that lasted a thousand years. Left: the Basilica of St. Peter's in St. Peter's Square, the focal point of the Roman Catholic Church and the most imposing church in Christendom. Below left: the Arch of Constantine, built in 315, and (bottom left) the Trevi Fountain, the largest, most splendid Roman fountain. Below: the Spanish Steps in front of the church of Trinità dei Monti, and (overleaf) Castel Sant' Angelo.

Above left and facing page bottom: the Colosseum, almost 2,000 years old and one of the most famous sites in Rome, and (left and below) the Roman Forum, even older than the nearby Colosseum and once the political center of ancient Rome. Above: Tibernia, an island in the middle of the River Tiber linked to the bank by the Fabrician Bridge, the only ancient Roman bridge in the city to survive the centuries intact. Below left: the Garden of the Vestal Virgins, Rome, and (facing page top) St. Peter's Square in Vatican City.

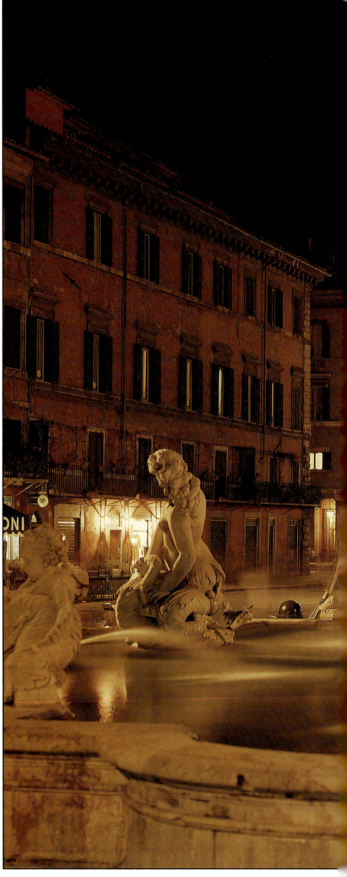

Rome (these pages and overleaf) shines at night with added glamor. Left: the Spanish Steps, a meeting place night and day, (below) Navona Square, where Neptune tussles with a monster amid fountains gilded in the floodlights, and (below left) liquid light in St. Peter's Square, where the highlighted dome of the great church – the largest in the world – towers over all. Bottom left: the Colosseum, and (overleaf) a storm breaks over the ruins of the temples of Vespasianus and Saturn.

Facing page top and above right: Positano, formerly a fishing village and now a resort on the Amalfi Drive, a road which follows the beautiful Amalfi coast south of Naples from Positano to Salerno. It is held that Ravello (facing page bottom) is the loveliest of the resorts along this coast, though nearby Atrani (above) also has its attractions. Below: the Marina Grande on the Isle of Capri, and (below right) Porto Sannazzaro in Mergellina. Right: the ruins of Pompeii.

Above: the sea licks the entrance to the Furore Valley, an awe-inspiring part of the Amalfi coast where the steep cliffs are often battered by wild seas. Amalfi itself (below and facing page) enjoys great popularity among Neapolitans as a retreat from the stresses of their city. Atrani (below left), also on the Amalfi coast, lies at the mouth of a rocky gorge. It is smaller and quieter than Amalfi. Left: Vietri Sul Mare, which clings to a cliff at the eastern end of the coast, and (above left) the village of Scilla on the southwestern toe of Italy.

Left: the Greek Temple of Concord, one of the best preserved of its kind in the world, at Agrigento on Sicily (these pages and overleaf). Below left: indomitable Messina, which has suffered many earthquakes during its history and was bombed during the Second World War, but which remains a thriving port, and (below) Taormina, near Mount Etna. Bottom left: the Cathedral of St. Agata in Catania, and (overleaf) Mondello, near the capital, Palermo. Following page: the major resort town of Sorrento.